Enviro-Sheltering

Enviro-Sheltering

Timothy McBride

ISBN 978-1-4583-2095-7

Table of Contents

CHAPTER THREE

Concepts of Enviro-Sheltering

* PHOTOVOLTAIC WATER PUMP FOR LIFESTOCK
* SOLAR GREEN HOUSE VS ATTACHED GREEN HOUSE
* WIND MACHINE ELECTRICAL POWER PLANT
* PHOTOVOLTAIC ELECTRICAL POWER PLANT
* GREEN HOUSE FARMING
* WATCH DOGS
* SOLAR HOT WATER COLLECTOR
* HOT WATER HEATING FIREPLACE
* SUNSPACE
* HYDROGEN FUEL CELL
* TOTAL ELECTRIC POWERED AUTOMOBILE
* SOLAR POWERED SUBWAY STATION
* NATURAL SOLAR DAYLIGHTING TUBE
* LONG DISTANCE MAGNETIC LEVITATION TRANSIT
* SYSTEM ABOVE EXISTING HIGHWAY
* LOCALIZED MAGNETIC LEVITATION METRO TRANSPORTER

CHAPTER FOUR

Site Analysis

* EARTH BERMED ENVIRO-SHELTER
* FINDING TRUE SOUTH LOCATION
* ESTABLISHING THE FOUR DIRECTIONS
* MID DAY SUN'S PATH BETWEEN SUMMER AND WINTER
* ESTABLISHING A SOLAR WINDOW
* LIVING WITH THE FOREST
* GLOBAL CLIMATE CHANGE
* SUN EARTH HEAT RELATIONSHIP
* SOLAR WATER PUMPING STATIONS
* COOLING TUBES
* SOLAR POWERED WATER FOUNTAIN
* RADIANT FLOORING
* PHOTOVOLTAIC POWERED WATER WELL PUMPING STATON

Chapter Five

Temporary to Permanent Shelters

* R V WITH SOLAR ELECTRIC MODULE SYSTEM
* MOUNTAIN SIDE SOLAR HYDRO POWER STATION
* WATER WELL, SOIL LEVELS AND BED ROCK
* WIND POWERED ELECTRICAL SYSTEM
* BIO-DIESEL PUMPING STATION
* SOLAR POWERED IRRIGATION AND LIFESTOCK WATERING STATION
* PORTABLE SOLAR SHOWER
* SOLAR SHOWER DESIGN
* THERMOSYPHON SOLAR HOT WATER COLLECTOR SYSTEM
* SOLAR CLOTHES DRYER
* SOLAR HOT WATER SHOWER STALL
* THERMO CONTROLLED PV POWERED ATTIC VENT
* SOLAR DISTILLER
* SOLAR OVEN SOLAR DEHYDRATOR
* SOLAR-ELECTRIC COOLING AND HEATING SUN STATION
* 12/24 VOLT DC POWERED CIRCULATOR PUMP

Chapter Six

Transportation and Manufacturing Within the Solar Nation

* INTERNATIONAL SOLAR COMPETITIONS
* ELECTRIC VEHICLES
* MAGNETIC LEVITATION TRACK SECTION
* SOLAR ELECTRIC POWER STATION
* D.C. POWERED CORDLESS RECHARGEABLE TOOL KIT
* A. C. TOOLS POWERED WITH THE AC INVERTER
* 2500 WATT DC TO AC INVERTER
* PASSIVE SOLAR TRACKER
* Solar Modular Home

The Emerging Solar Civilization

ENVIRO-SHELTERING

INTRODUCTION

Enviro-Sheltering is the study of humans effects on the natural environment at present, with new alternative ways of improving cause of more harmonious effects in the future. With this thought in mind. Just where does these effects begin and how can each individual do something on this level to change present trends that are very dangerous to all species of life now living on this planet? Considering the supply and demand system of our present economy, is it not the demand for the supply that actually drives the wheels of the industrial world? With diminishing supplies and increased demand the straw that breaks the camels back has already been thrown. In fact crushed. Also the trade-off expense to our natural environment is actually cutting the life line of our very existence. What to do about these life threatening advances are keeping the thinking minds of our society in a constant mode of problem solving in which the collective imaginations are being stretched to their limits. For these and many other reasons the concepts of these writings are being kept to be considered as possible alternatives.

CHAPTER ONE

Contrasting Ecologies

On the one hand we have mankind with their well-known struggles to maintain the environment they choose to build around themselves. On the other hand we have nature with all the natural forces at work to use the land for its means. The ones seems to be in constant battle with the other. Now with a closer look at these builders let's see how each work together or apart. We have undoubtedly obtained the power to manipulate certain forces in nature for so called productive purposes. But we must remember that these productive purposes are only productive in the eyes of the so-called beneficiary. Let's try to see the whole spectrum, because only then can we say we are studying the happenings in our environment. Nature being the servant is usually faithful to produce many new products. These products are then manufactured into the stuff of our modern societies. Needs and wants which in all reality is the supply of our convenient lifestyles. The natural systems are programmed to replenish themselves automatically, but always with a stress factor. Given any piece of ground with too much of a demand, it will soon reach it's stage of balance between give and take. As you can see nothing is actually free without trade-offs. Each of these trade-offs will either directly or indirectly effect us for better or for worse.

FOOD CHAINS

Eating is a favorite pastime for most life on this planet. Being the biological creatures that we are we are not a exemption to this task. Instead we stand at the top of a very very long strain of food parts beings passed up to us from other forms of life and in turn we use these items to build our inner structures of our bodies and their features. Now like any structure its well being is only as good as its component parts. So in all reality the better the parts the better the structure. Now the point we are trying to make here is that with the reality of the environmental trade-offs that directly effect the component parts coming to us, are we in truth destroying ourselves? Think about it. Now let's go into the next topic. But always remembering that we are living, Organisms. So we need live fresh locally grown food, air & water and sunshine,and community to maintain good health.

FLUIDS AND GASES

In nature we find many fluids and gases that are used every second to sustain our very life along with all other life as we know it. These fluids and gases encircle our world in large systems of flow and change as they inner react with different life forms. The compositional balance of these are crucial to all life. As we add alien, (man made pollutants) fluids and gases to these systems, they take on stress factors.

In efforts to maintain its natural systems these stumbling blocks poise adverse effects on all life on this planet as we all know. Air, land, and water, air and noise pollution has been around for quite a while now. With the present accelerated rate of change in the composition of our atmosphere. How readily can we adapt to altered environments, or perish?

ENERGY

As we all know by now energy is everywhere and anywhere in many different forms and shapes. We have many ways of tapping into these energies to give the power to animate modern civilization as we know it today. Yet it is through the apprehension of these energies that many harmful effects to the environment occur, not only is energy transported vast distances but energy is used to transport many other products around the globe. Most all of this movement of matter is brought about for the sole purpose of our desire to live with a urban convenient society. A closer look at this lifestyle will uncover the unsettling reality that our convenience is enjoyed only at the expense of many other facets of life and life-sustaining substances. These trends if left unchecked will eventually cut off the lifeline of humanity itself.

HUMAN RELATIONS

With these factors of environmental degeneration we now stand at the threshold either to wake up and face the facts that we and our whole environment are part of a very close closed integrated system that cannot exist without our stewardship any more than we can exist without it working properly with all the natural life sustaining systems intact. The truth of the matter lies in the one fact that even our very thoughts play havoc with these natural forces bending them and shaping them into the reality of our world. As so to start changing thought patterns with the existing patterns of nature will result in a new outlook as to how we could learn to, live on this planet. Only you and I can do this with a burning desire to change our world into something beautiful and self-sustaining and then act on our dreams as goals to reality.

CHAPTER TWO

The Rising Horizon

Possibly unknown to the general public many wonderful advances has been set into action to detour or slow down the ever present accelerate rate of desolation to this planet. The fact is many environmental clean-up projects has successfully benefited in reducing stress factors on the natural ecosystem. Nevertheless, the roots of the problems have not been tackled therefore these advances are only temporary fixes. In fact in the overall review the real problem has been missed entirely.

This is the problem of the way most humans live in their homes along with this planet. Now the cat's out of the bag. Our homes or better yet our immediate habitats, or simply our Enviro-Shelters. For one reason is the fact that our conventional homes are usually only energy consumers in every respect. They give us the needed requirement of food, entertainment, shelter, and comfort with a price tag too large for most people. Even those who do indulge, soon find that the time away from the house keeps growing longer as the bills begin to roll in. After some time the lady of the house goes to work to help out. This means a extra car, more insurance, if children, day care, added gas expense, even more insurance, less time to manage household adding to more stress and which soon adds more medical expenses, not considering loss of education and the sense of family. With these conditions in mind with the fact that most of these problems go back and hinge on the fact that the so-called modern home is an expensive uneconomical way to live. So for many people it is back to the drawing board to figure out what has gone wrong. Now it is hard to grasp the full picture of the magnitude of this problem, and the solution is sometimes even harder to grasp without advancing to higher levels of thought. But these levels can be reached by taking the time to look at ourselves for what we really are, and by recognizing where we came from, and where we could go. Accepting one important fact that nothing in the past can help us in the future except the experience of having been there. Realizing that we are the problem. Accept that and move forward into the solution. Only living in the realm of the solution with thoughts and actions can preservation be realized and restoration begin. The restoration we are speaking of, is the movement back to a harmonious rapport with nature, nature's ways, nature's laws, nature's loving care and sheltering kindness.

With these and many other motivations the Southern Enviro-Shelter Project is begun to plant seeds of success and growth towards implementation of alternative and renewable energies until it merges with similar projects to eventually engulf the whole globe with unity and harmony with all life. With this dream this chapter ends on the note that all life is interwoven into a complex system of interdependence and each internal part must be cherished and preserved to maintain the whole.

CHAPTER THREE

Concepts of Enviro-Sheltering

The overall purpose of the shelter in discussion is to draw around itself all necessities of human life with the least adverse effects to the natural environment. This in turn means an intensive study of the natural environment to find ways in which we can benefit it while it benefits us. This kind of cooperation with nature will involve many automatic systems for at close study nature is full of automation. With this in mind many desired results can be set up to trigger flow systems that are integrated in unison with those of nature. A flow system is using a natural occurrence to trigger a response in another direction to benefit a need without altering the natural occurrence.

PHOTOVOLTAIC WATER PUMP FOR LIFESTOCK

For example, directing roof top run-off rainwater into a greenhouse for irrigation thru a closed cistern to enhance the growth of plants, enhance the air supply and food supply with a delay in rain, a moisture sensor relay to activate a photo electric pump to move water to plants with desired intervals, with excess heat from greenhouse back to the living space or heating water for use. The excess overflow water lines to livestock and fish ponds with animal and plant compost back to greenhouse and gardens to enhance growth of plants. Notice the flow of this mini ecological system within its small circle. there are many many systems like this in nature, But notice with humans added technology the light entered the system to pump water when times of no rain although in which times there is usually much sunlight. We will be using many systems like this in the shelter which will add up to a totally self-sufficient habitat with an animated life of its own.

SOLAR GREEN HOUSE VS ATTACHED GREEN HOUSE

Another example, A large oak tree is naturally situated to block incoming sun rays from the southwest on hot summer days the the shade of this tree is much cooler air than the neighboring exposed air. Just by locating a large glass area at this shaded point will bring in a soft Light during summer but in the winter as the leaves fall the sunlight comes beaming through to light or heat space or water inside shelter. The fallen leaves in turn serve as mulch for the flower beds gardens which enhance beauty, bee honey and food.

Notice the technology here is the glass which traps the heat to benefit plants, and animals inside the shelter with trade-offs going back to benefit the natural system. These mini-ecosystems will soon begin to carry over into the others this overlapping only ensures the efficiency of the overall program. As we will soon see a type of music will begin to play to the rhythm of nature when every occurrence will cause a response within the system of our environment.

WIND MACHINE ELECTRICAL POWER PLANT

Another example, On a windy day the pollen is being moved through the air. A cool breeze is being moved through the wild flower garden shelter, seeds are landing everywhere from these mothering plants and the wind charger is moving electrons into the battery bank the program turns on the sound system and we hear some beautiful music all throughout, while we read our way to peaceful sleep by the glow of our cluster white diode lighting system. During the night a cloud is being blown in with a burst of rain to raise the level of the neighboring stream to accelerate the water wheel alternator to charge batteries and refill the watering tanks and small ponds. The rushing of water over the ground has moved the upper layer of fertile manured soil from pastures to the lower level gardens where it is trapped by erosion barriers placed there by humans. Notice that the wind charger acted on by nature to bring the light, pump water and music. As well the erosion barriers stopped the compost at the right location to enhance plant growth. Of course the Human's main habitat can be quite a distance away from all this activity and other means could beam or translate the energy to the main living quarters such as natural-gas digesters.

For instance the energy can be piped under ground a long distance and for instance the electricity from a wind generator can be wired underground.

PHOTOVOLTAIC ELECTRICAL POWER PLANT

Another example— With a wonderful sunrise a sunbeam catches my eye from the easterly faced glazing, as shadows dot my face from the reflection of the house plants. I arise to notice the amp meter pegged by the incoming energy from the photo electric modules mounted on the roof above me. This gives me the assurance that my early morning shop chores are intact with plenty of electricity . From the living room I look southward to notice the surge in growth in the plants with renewed water, fertilizer, and sunshine, a fresh fragrance of air fills my lungs.

GREEN HOUSE FARMING

I noticed fresh garden vegetables ready to be picked. After breakfast I will head out to build that enclosed kitchen gazebo over the outdoor living space where food preparation keeps unwanted smells and soils out of the main living quarters lowering cleaning chores for all. In the meantime while working with the chicken pen I noticed the mother hen sitting on her eggs so I skipped over her while gathering the rest. Stepping out into the yard the trough was running over with water from filtered rainwater. The chickens were scratching in the leaves where table and garden scraps where left there from the day before. Couldn't help but notice how their scratching would blend their own droppings into a compost mixture perfect for plant growth.

I noticed the program had switched the automatic gates to allow the birds more grazing area which also works great for weed and bug control especially under fruit trees and vineyards where the droppings and scratching benefits their livelihood. The keepers come over to let me know that all has went well through the night. The keepers are two large German shepherds who have access to all areas thru special gates.

WATCH DOGS

Time to milk so as we go into the barn noticing the sludge pump needs a few more shovels of manure for methane production underground in the digester which powers back up generators and tractors and other farm equipment. The spent sludge is pumped into the compost pile near the gardens. We are set for another week. Finally with corn from the bin we start to milk the cow. Finishing the milking chore she is turned out into a new grazing area where fresh grass have grown . We returned to the processing shelter with milk, eggs, and vegetables along with fresh berries and fruits.

SOLAR HOT WATER COLLECTOR

Another example- On a cool winter day as we prepare to build a fire from select hard woods from the northern forest I activate a program that controls water valves to activate the solar assisted thermosiphon heat collection tubes located in the stove which stores hot water in a super insulated tank in the attic. After the heat energy reaches a preset temperature a photovoltaic circulation fan activates to move the warm air throughout the shelter. The hot air that rises to the ceiling of the exposed beams where a duct pulls the hot air away to the greenhouse to help assist the incoming heat from the glazing. This process is reversed when the sun's more intense heat is drawn from the greenhouse into the shelter where a air/water heat exchanger acts to replace the tanks with hot water during the day when the fire dies down or on hot days sometimes the excess heat is simply vented into the atmosphere by thermal actuator vents.

HOT WATER HEATING FIREPLACE

The migration from the outside gardens is almost complete at this time of the year except for certain plants that can survive the winter in hot beds or on southern ends of the farm when sunlight and the animals' body heat help keep them alive with some input from the methane burners on extremely cold days. The upper portion of all the farm buildings are designed to support plant life because the heat is trapped in these areas against insulation. Also special dug-outs in south-faced hills with glazed tops support plant life, with help from the earth-farming effects. The efforts put into these projects pay off quickly because canning and food preserving is cut down considerably and replaced with fresh-picked foods. The extra nutritional valve also adds vitality with stimulated health and energy.

SUNSPACE

With the arrival of spring the seedlings started early in the greenhouse greatly accelerate the harvest time especially now that the animals have prepared the land all winter with cultivation and fertilizer. With the changing of the season the winds have accelerated to bring more power input from the wind charger. So on this particular day with plenty of photoelectric input to the hydrogen /solar electric car, it is charged to its full potential. Which means an adventurous 600 mile drive through the country to visit friends in the neighborhood of Utopian ECO Village. As we go out the door the monitor system is activated to watch over the shelters while we are away with remote controls in the automobile we can accomplish many chores if our stay away is extended. Upon arrival to our friends house we plug into the visitors socket to recharge for the trip back home. By the way everybody has visitor sockets and it is common courtesy to share solar energy with all travelers.

HYDROGEN FUEL CELL VS

TOTAL ELECTRIC POWERED AUTOMOBILE

On the large national transit systems for long distance travel where you leave your electric car at the station and use courtesy vehicles at your temporary destination.

Some of these large transit systems are run on magnetic impulses from electronic magnets that repel them down a track made for floatation restraint others run off direct solar drives just like solar cars. The view from these tracks are great with Enviro-Shelters, In full bloom this time of year. It is all the Enviro-Shelters along the way that power the trains thru the solar grid interconnected villages. Since the Shelters of the future are self-sufficient that releases a heavy load off the utility grids such as large hydro-electric dams to produce hydrogen fuel for mass transit systems between cities along the man made lake systems across the country.

NATURAL-GAS POWERED SUBWAY STATION

Another example- As you may have noticed by now there is little non-organic waste in the Enviro-Shelter, therefore all waste is returned to nature as feed for animals or fertilizer for plants or fuel for domestic purposes. The systems that control these wastes are either automatic or conveniently located to ease the flow of the recyclables and biodegradables. All non-organic wastes are returned to special recycle stations for reprocessing. There are no land fills any more for this source is used as fuel for public transits between populated centers.

NATURAL SOLAR DAYLIGHTING TUBE

Natural day lighting to bring in the sunlight with sky lights, windows, mirrors and optics is essential in key areas where design and position being built into the structure. These areas are backed up by lighting systems that are sensitive to the changing light density of the room.

They only activate when someone enters the room and only then if incoming sunlight doesn't meet the required lighting requirements. Insulated blankets with beautiful designs are automatically activated to lower or raise in front of the large south-facing glazing on tracks to control solar heat gain or loss. These not only hold in radiant heat at night but also act as a light and heat control during the day with thermostatic controls.

LONG DISTANCE MAGNETIC LEVITATION

TRANSIT SYSTEM ABOVE EXISTING HIGHWAY

Today while sitting under the big eastern oak noticing the buds burst forth with new life as the fragrance from early spring wild flowers greet the morning sky. A new beginning, the feeling of freedom flowing greatly through my mind. This sparks a wonderful new idea that begins to germinate within and grows into maturity, a vision a full grown brainstorm.

LOCALIZED MAGNETIC LEVITATION

METRO TRANSPORTER

Utopia Eco-Village is a land full of happy people living in perfect peace with all the time in the world to build marvelous creations as if their imaginations are unleashed forever with the love for all life gently flowing through the endless seas of timeless bliss.

“ The wolf dwelled with the lamb. The lion ate straw like the ox. There was no hurt in the whole land.”

With so much tranquility people were building dwellings with intensive care not to harm or destroy but to blend in with welcome unity as all the living creations moved around to envelope them. The citizens are floating on air with devices using magnetic levitation technology with can be adapted to almost any vehicle now that the very asphalt is magnetically coated with photovoltaic substrate surfaces. The solar highways are almost complete everywhere. Crafts are buzzing around like insects on the wind.

CHAPTER FOUR

Site Analysis

This chapter will start the beginners, those who wish to travel the road to a more self-sufficient lifestyle and adventure into the solar age. Always remember that these precepts are for multiple climates, but as we move to other locations on our globe, different environmental factors come in to play, therefore everything has to be considered and taken into account. Site analysis is simply what it says analyzing a piece of ground over a period of time to discern certain aspects about the property. These apprehensions will begin to pop into your mind with a face of your own creativity. The following is only a guideline to possibly help towards a desired path.

Balance and harmony will flow together only with the feelings of when it is right for ones on self. This alone will mean that each Enviro-Shelter will have unique characteristics of the over-flowing spirits inhabiting them. Each mind in its perception of nature will differ greatly. For this reason the special engineers that design these sites must develop a rapport with the humans they are serving, as well the natural environment and other lifeforms plant or animal that surround them at the site for development. These special designers we are speaking of have experience with all flow systems with adept knowledge of the workings of the Bio-systems within nature. This working knowledge will have grown with proof of hands on experience and applied wisdom inside oneself to a high level of competence and skill. This knowing must be flowing out with great eagerness to know more, letting the imagination encircle higher levels of thought without fear.

EARTH BERMED ENVIRO-SHELTER

The Enviro- Shelter Designer/Engineer must be able to envision the entire structure in every detail holding thoughts committing them to paper and pictures. Time is timeless in the minds of these — set no limits for they must work without restrictions on their natural talents. Their reward is in helping others therefore all their basic needs must be met in full. Ask questions freely as they come to mind upon setting up the site. The site preparation will begin to blend into the natural lay of the land as well the local climate. If you have the time to sit and watch a true Solar Enviro-Shelter engineer at work these things just might occur.

(First day) — After greetings with small talk soon the conversation would drift to the available optional lands and desireables, upon this a move to a comfortable distance to observe the site from several perspectives. Just for clarification lets say the proposed, SESDE Person, (Solar Enviro-Shelter Designer/Engineer) after sitting for hours on each spot her mind has narrowed down two best optimal as well positional locations for the shelters radius point of evolution. She takes up mental residence at one of the chosen locations and breaks out the solar mechanics tool box of magic and sets up shop, then begins collecting data about the site and makes notes and rough drawings. Within several hours, she has a basic outline of various shelters and out buildings. She takes photographs of the site and stakes out the four directions north,east,west and south as well the basic contour of the property. The following is one way to determine the true south direction of a site always remember that compass magnetic south is not always true south.

FINDING TRUE SOUTH LOCATION

A note, On a sunny day then make notes for time of sunrise as well sunset. Now calculate to the exact time of day that is between these two times. For instance if the sunrise is 6:00 AM and the sunset is at 6:00 PM then the halfway point would be 12:00 noon.

In this case at 12:00 noon place a stake in the shadow of the first stake some distance further south. The line that is drawn between the stake under the plumb bob to the shadow stake is true south. The opposite direction is North and the right angle from this line towards sunset is west then of course the right angle towards the sunrise is east.

ESTABLISHING THE FOUR DIRECTIONS

The next step is to put ribbons on any trees or note any structure that may block solar access to the site. It only takes a fist-sized chunk of shade to effectively turn off a PV module or render a hot water collector less effective. Wondering if that tree or building will shade your array during certain times of the year?

MID DAY SUN'S PATH BETWEEN SUMMER AND WINTER

Then she begins listing all the native or natural resources existing on the site as well the overall condition of vegetation and soil and water and air as well existing animal or insect residents if any on the site as well erosion. After she has collected enough data she begins to refine her data and drawings. She will present the owners or developers with her basic plans the following day, or after she has done her homework. Trees that are considerably bent or diseased or dead are tagged with color ribbons for careful removal. By now the sun Is reaching the peaks of the western trees in which are tagged as being blockers, (keep notes)

ESTABLISHING A SOLAR WINDOW

Some of these tagged blocker trees are only so at this time of the year but this gives us a reference point to calculate other blockers. Additional photographs are also taken with extreme care to show the land flow as well where shadows are cast on the ground. Photos from the center to east, west, north, and south and from each of these directions inward. Upon completion of this the rest of the day is spent working up an essay for the general layout for in fact each site has it's own biography. Many web sites offer information on how to get local statistics of weather patterns especially the average rain fall and average wind speeds but each site will have a micro-climate that is unique to that site only.
(Day Two)

LIVING WITH THE FOREST

Upon arrival back to the site this new data is worked into the site charts. Next a hole is dug in various areas to determine percolation as well, to find out average depth of topsoil sand clay or rock. After this the proposed site for the water well if needed and septic system is located and placed on the drawings. If a stream exists on the site or if a man-made stream is chosen to be made the flow rate is calculated into gallons of water per minute. Alternate paths or channels are drawn to project water into various areas of the shelter for either sound, views or practical purpose.

Waterfalls and ponds are also proposed in areas where the land can accept these without excess digging or movement of soil like in slopes, depths, or hollows. Planned strategy for all run-off water is also proposed to accent useful purposes for practical reasons. Some of these will have more importance for your landscaping plans than others. If there is a stream on your property, you will need to know the extent of its floodplain and unless you plan to build, you will not be concerned with the foundation strength of your bedrock. All this data is formulated into sketches to be used later in working drawings and as always be sure to consult local professionals about any building codes and or regulations. In long time desolate sites where the natural cycles of life and change have been altered by the damming up of normal flow of organic cause and effects will be a much greater challenge to restore to Enviro-Shelter status with proper solar orientation and vitality. The spreading of asphalt and concrete over vast regions of the earth's surface has undoubtedly played havoc with certain of these forces with further input to other factors occurring simultaneously has pushed the ever-present need for Enviro-Sheltering to be considered in a global manner.

GLOBAL CLIMATE CHANGE

This higher level of consideration will bring a more holistic view of the organic living planet Earth into the proper perspective as the ultimate site for human existence or other planets engineered by organic terraforming methods learned here on our home planet.

Wither you believe in climate change or not it still doesn't relieve you of the responsibility of the stewardship of your immediate environment. No matter what we need to prepare ourselves for the extremes of the seasons anyway, regardless of what happens.

SUN EARTH HEAT RELATIONSHIP

But our concern now is the piece of ground on the surface of the earth in which we are to extract, inhale, consume, exhaust our immediate existence. Land which in the past has been taken for granted that out there will exist forever a supply. The chain of vital goods, but during this circle the substances are returned back to nature damaged at the unresponsive handling at the present state of technology.

SOLAR WATER PUMPING STATIONS

Imagine that we lived in a civilization where each individual was responsible for the protection of his or her own space of existence. The space of existence is the clean air we need for life the healthy food and drink we need around us for healthy bodies and minds. We all know how long any of us can live without their vital elements. Also most streams contain fish. Simple rock, earth, concrete and timber can be used to dam streams to begin aquaculture projects onto and within the site.

COOLING TUBES

The cool water also may be used for the cooling of the shelters by circulating it into coils inside floors either by gravity or photoelectric powered pumps. The water releasing its cooling nature to the shelter by photovoltaic fans blowing across coils or by natural up drafts. Also starting with direct solar powered ventilator, and a well insulated attic, and reflective roofing. The idea is that a cool attic helps keep a cool house and is central to keeping a house more comfortable, and also helps keep a fresh stream of air flowing through the house on the hotter days when usually the sun source is active to operate the devices counteracting the Sun's effect. The idea is not to create a trap for the rising hot air but instead channeling the hot air into the atmosphere or hot air to water heat exchanger to preheat water before entering the solar collector already located on the roof.

SOLAR POWERED WATER FOUNTAIN

A very fun water project with solar is the fountain and can be accomplish several ways using a submersible direct solar powered pump with a nozzle created for the desired effect. The raised or warmed water can be used for refill pre-heating tanks, radiant floors, irrigation pools, or other water projects, or simply returned to the stream using a solar fountain.

RADIANT FLOORING

Considering the estimated annual global mean temperature rise of our planet. The site of the temporary shelter is best located in the cool hardwoods if in southern climates, and earth bermed possibly on a north-facing slope for summer times. Another shelter on a south facing slope for winter time. Earth-buried cooling tubes are also an option to create a cool air draft from cooler air rising from the tubes inside the shelter space from a lower inlet draft from a shaded hardwood area. These tubes need to be at least six inches in diameter at levels below the grounds heating index or frost line.

PHOTOVOLTAIC POWERED WATER WELL PUMPING STATON

The temperature below the ground is usually between 62-68 degrees downwards to six feet below the surface . The length of tubes should be thirty to fifty feet to allow air flow time to cool down while drafting towards the shelter space. To reclaim land that has a barrier of concrete, asphalt, trash, or just plain barren waste land back to vitality again, will involve much care. First the debris must not be cycled from the site in a way while diverting the same problem for your neighbors or another site elsewhere wither land fills are legal or not. The buck passing of solid liquid and or toxic waste stops here. First analyze all debris and make a inventory list this will prove very helpful later in the project.

Which is recyclable? do some research. Use! Some may even be helpful in establishing a materials shop with adjacent storage shed.

Chapter Five

Temporary to Permanent Shelters

A temporary shelter is one that protects human life, animals, plants or materials from the elements while a better more solid stable structure is being built. The temporary or transitional shelter can be a very efficient area for planning and development of the site. A sort of workshop with sleeping areas if need be and eating areas. If preferred a separate structure for eating, preserving, or preparing foods. A small geodesic dome, RV, trailer, barn, metal storage, or simple log structure can be easy to construct and demand less time and energy. Renting a existing nearby house during construction is also a good option.

The shelter will become the focus point from which the site will begin to manifest itself. It also can serve as a prefabrication site as well material storage. Each day must be devoted to playful yet serious work. The greenhouse, garden projects should be started as soon as possible. First for food replenishment and of course to establish a edible landscape. On most undeveloped sites, if still fertile with the organic process already at work? Lucky you, take the time to check out the existing plant growth. For instance in my area we have hickory trees, muscadine vines, black berries, elder berries walnut trees and blue berries, poke salad and many others herbs and others that are native and come up naturally. Try not to destroy food-producing native plants. If these should be growing already where the temporary shelter is to be built, water and fertilize the ground around the plants, or transplant them into the desired areas and further fertilize to enhance growth and yield. Using mulch and animal manures, called composing and mulching. Compost bins are to be constructed out of rocks and logs or dirt and lumber. These should be located some distance from the shelter usually at the edges or centers of garden sites.

R V WITH SOLAR ELECTRIC MODULE SYSTEM

Once the temporary shelter is in place the other more permanent animal and human shelters can begin as materials time and ability is acquired. Most streams supply a portion of sand, clay, gravel, water and rock and hopefully fish. Some even have pottery clay or a potential power to do work from a small hydro-electric plant or just a water wheel. Decay, rot and rust is usually at work on a site enhancing to speed up the process of decomposing.

Adding more already decomposing materials like fallen trees, leaves,or animal waste. Encourage earthworms,and microbes that speed up the decaying process. In time plant rapid-growing coverage that will thrive on the decayed material bringing it into the living plant organism and re releasing its matter to the environment. Into a new birth and atmosphere. the land is reclaimed, the normal process of Enviro-Sheltering can begin and new processes started as well importation of vegetation onto the site. Streams also need to be tested for water purity. Start by hiking to the head of your stream to see if any discharge or run-off may be entering at some point upstream. Note the washes on hill sides that enter the stream. If a potential problem is occurring begin at once to set in motion the energy for correction for water is a vital resource as we all know.

MOUNTAIN SIDE SOLAR HYDRO POWER STATION

A well also is an option for a site and the rope pulley and bucket will bring the water to you until the windmill or photovoltaic pumping system installed, but first the well has to be dug or drilled. Hydro-electric generator is dependent on the flow of water through the site or heavy rainfall in the guttering system. The amount of water falling is measured in gallons per minute or running pounds of pressure. This amount will vary greatly from different sites. There will be variation from dry to wet weather seasons. We will illustrate the varied electrical supply in amps with the average use patterns of a region's wet season, which is usually the spring or fall time of the year.

Water falling with a running pressure of 40 pounds will yield a steady 24 hour electrical charge to the battery bank at 10 amps. The extra water can be used for a storage cistern for irrigation or other domestic purposes, such as a fountain or a waterfall. The electricity can also we used to operate DC well pumps directly or other fun water projects.

WATER WELL, SOIL LEVELS AND BED ROCK

The site for a well is usually chosen in a area where it is close to the shelter or possibly below the floor of the future well house shelter chosen by the Dowser. This way the pumps and pipes will be protected from freezing. The method of digging the well of course will depend on the equipment available to you. Hopefully in the near future Bio-Diesel or Solar-powered well drilling rigs will be commonplace.

WIND POWERED ELECTRICAL SYSTEM

Most wind charger will begin charging batteries with a 8 mph breeze or a wind machine can also pump water directly. Wind power comes in many variations such as wind speed, direction, temperature, height, gusty, or smooth. This of course changes with the seasons making wind energy hard to predict but mostly is blowing during seasonal changes.

Some wind sites have a prevailing wind that is fairly constant year round. Air flow is less turbulent and more steady 5 feet above tree line. Also a good power tower can be used to mount photovoltaic modules, water tanks, solar collectors, and communication devices, etc....

BIO-DIESEL PUMPING STATION

Methane (Natural gas-Bio-gas or Wood- gas) powered motor driven alternator is a unique way to disperse organic waste. Twenty pounds of dry matter which consists of dry leaves, vegetable scraps, straw, and activated sludge will yield 250 cubic feet of biological gas. This gas can be used to run engines, cook, light, refrigerate, boil water, etc. The gas produced when sludge is piped underground to a storage digester for on demand fuel use when needed. Personal use patterns illustrate the consumption rate per hour with various burn tasks. A 1 horsepower combustion engine will consume 18 cubic feet biological gas per hour coupled with a 2000 Watts D.C. 110 volt generator. The generator will produce 1860 Watts while running on biological gas. The generator set on automatic demand during high human use pattern periods. Generator peak demand back up with human use patterns for all seasons, as well a natural gas converter system on the average car will allow this system to refuel hybrid automobiles at the local household station.

SOLAR POWERED IRRIGATION

AND LIFESTOCK WATERING STATION

Okay! Now of course our water system needs a means of pressurization so here again we have chosen to use a simple solar energy design to accomplish this means. A solar powered pumping system is basically a 12 Volt or 24 volt, Direct Current pump that uses direct sunlight to activate the pumping cycle. The water is raised into a tank that is elevated above all other domestic water systems as to advantage the extra pressure by using gravity to push the water to outlet water systems either hot or cold either day or night all around the habitat. Many Solar Farmsteads will have local utility water available at a meter and this is a option to tap into even though you may not want to drink the water or pay a water bill. Anyway to invest in your own water system will be cheaper than bottled water or utility water over the long haul with less waste.

PORTABLE SOLAR SHOWER

The next subject to be considered is the shower area or bath. A shower house or stall can be constructed very quickly on the site and should allow for adequate hygiene and clothes washing as well drying. All these chores can be accomplished using solar hot water collectors with a super insulated storage tank located several feet above the shower head or using a photovoltaic pump.

If a well or water supply isn't easily available then a rain water cistern can be incorporated into the system to collect strained rain water. Since rain water is falling from the sky already above the habitat there is no need to use extra energy to pump it around so we suggest to collect the rain water at the highest elevation possible usually a few inches below the roof gutters or inside the attic. The cistern can be plumbed into toilets, exterior wash and cleaning basins, irrigation or other domestic water destinations. Once we have accumulated our dependable water supply we can begin to get creative with some really nice water projects such as a solar heated hot tub, solar fountains, waterfalls, garden streams, small ponds and swimming pools etc.

SOLAR SHOWER DESIGN

A modern very efficient washing machine can be operated off an photovoltaic array and a AC inverter. If you are using a old fashioned clothes line. Both should be working well in full sunshine. I'm not just advocating you do washing chores just on sunny days.
Hot and cold water is one of the most important aspects of the modern world not only for hygiene but for many household uses and is expected as common in these times. So we have begun our system with the quest for water. The units we have chosen to use are thermosyphon systems because not only are they the simplest to construct but uses the least amount of energy to create hot water. The basic rule that hot water rises is used within these solar systems to activate the heater only when the sun source is there to circulate without pumps, and heats without any electricity or gas from other sources.

Convection moves heated liquid upwards in the system as it is simultaneously replaced by cooler liquid returning by gravity. Ideally, the liquid flows easily because a good thermosiphon should have very little hydraulic resistance. To keep the water hot during nights and cloudy days the tank is super insulated inside the attic area. For freeze protection of the collectors themselves they also can be located inside the attic space under a large south facing skylight.

THERMOSYPHON SOLAR HOT WATER COLLECTOR SYSTEM

The storage tank, located above the collector receives heated water coming from the top of the collector into the top of the storage tank. Colder water from the bottom of the storage tank will be drawn into the lower entry of the solar collector to replace the heated water that was thermosyphoned upward. The storage tank may or may not use a heat exchanger. The thermosyphon system is more costly and complex than the batch system. In our area, it is best to use an indirect system (one that employs a heat exchanger). In that case, antifreeze can be used in the system eliminating freeze ups. This type system loacted in attic area and super insulated can save hot water for many cloudy days with some input from a wood heater's hot water coils.

SOLAR CLOTHES DRYER

Even rainy days are good for washing. Using a simple water wheel and filtered rain water to do the chore. In fact clothes can be hung up in a special closet in upper portion of a shelter with a drain pan as it's floor. The warm rising air from the shelter vented into this closet will simply drip dry your clothes on rainy days. Clean clothes are a must and people all over the world have become accustom to the concept of a machine to wash and dry their clothes and expect this technology to continue into the future. Okay, a traditional clothes line has been in use since time immortal and this basic concept of hanging clothes out in the sunshine is still a very efficient cheap way to dry clothes, but is there still a better way? Lets Explore some possibilities of the total solar powered laundry. Here we have done some experimenting with a solar chamber that acts as a clothes cleaning closet. When exchanging clothes simply hang the used pair into the solar closet and activate the cycle. Once the clothes are scoured with solar heated hot water through pressure nozzles the clothes will drip dry towards the floor grate drain as solar pre-heated air is circulated thru the chamber or in some designs a skylight is installed. Futuristic fabrics can be designed to accent this type of solar cleaning. You will find below some links to some interesting innovations we have found that look very promising technologies or easily incorporated into the solar electric laundry systems of the future.

SOLAR HOT WATER SHOWER STALL

Another option rather than using a modern water closet is to install a composting toilet. These devices are very efficient at disposing human waste without using water and in some cases without electricity. These also eliminate the need for expensive septic tanks and field lines. We will now discuss several of these methods and introduce you to, Composting Toilet World.

Composting Toilet World is an advocate for the use of composting toilets worldwide. Our goal is to educate, promote and facilitate the use of compost toilets. Well now that we have all our basic creature comforts intact, lets move onto the next discussion. Sleeping, eating, entertaining, and study areas are very important places not only for the human being but also for the human spirit. In today's world most people are used to their electronics and are surrounded by them.

I'm talking music, pods, cells, players, dvd players, televisions,telephones,computers as well other personals such as flashlights,electronic game players, electric shavers,coffee makers,blenders,can openers, refrigerators, microwave ovens, water and heat pumps and of course light fixtures and fans as well almost any modern appliance and electronic item can powered by natural energy systems.

THERMO CONTROLLED PV POWERED ATTIC VENT

All these devices have one thing in common they use electricity. Most actually use very little electricity, but some appliances use more such as the refrigerator and heat pump so we will talk about these separate from the others. A super insulated thick walled chamber is a very efficient refrigerator and freezer designed for solar electric applications is used in most cases. Refrigeration has been around for quite a while now from its humble beginnings of a simple ice box to now giant walk in coolers, freezers and HVAC systems. Many prototype solar powered heat pumps are making head way into the markets all over the world.

SOLAR DISTILLER

A fresh water supply is a concern for all humans as more contaminates are finding their way into the river, streams, and aquifers. A simple solar distiller device can easily provide gallons of fresh water for drinking and cooking. These units can be designed to be plumbed into a south facing kitchen area or simply incorporated on the south facing roof and gravity fed anywhere in the habitat below. Energy from the sun heats water inside the still to the point of evaporation. Water vapor rises, condenses on the inner glass surface of the still, and drips into a collection tank. This process removes impurities such as salts and heavy metals as well as eliminates microbiological organisms.

What we are concerned with here basically is food preservation and human comfort so lets start will a well insulated passive solar living space with a old fashioned pantry for storage of dry goods, seeds,seasonings,herbs, and canned goods and the like. Store as much of your food stocks in this very tight sealed area in good containers.

SOLAR OVEN SOLAR DEHYDRATOR

Adjacent to this area towards the south should be another area for a solar distiller, a solar oven, and solar dehydrator, and of course the BBQ. Okay! In thermodynamic terms, the two driving forces in the universe are a simultaneous tendency for less enthalpy and more entropy. Tending to less enthalpy is to cool down and dissipate heat. Tending to more entropy is to become random and free. Personally, I strive for less tension and more freedom, although sometimes I must compromise one for the other. And that is what water is doing in an evaporator cooler. The quest for freedom on a molecular level is one of the two guiding forces in its physical existence. To gain the greater measure of entropy, it is willing to sacrifice a little enthalpy. Many Solar powered evaporator coolers are on the market now and work really well in arid climates. Here in the south, we have a lot of very high humidity days so many homes here use heat pumps. Always keep in mind that just by designing a super passive solar dwelling the active solar system will use a lot less energy and will mainly serve as backups to top off passive integrated solar systems for added comfort or another desired application.

SOLAR-ELECTRIC COOLING AND HEATING SUN STATION

Another good solar cooling application is the solar powered evaporating cooler. Evaporator cooling is a physical phenomenon in which evaporation of a liquid, typically into surrounding air, cools an object or a liquid in contact with it. Latent heat describes the amount of heat that is needed to evaporate the liquid; this heat comes from the liquid itself and the surrounding gas and surfaces. The greater the difference between the two temperatures, the greater the evaporate cooling effect. When using solar to directly power your evaporator cooler just use a D C Motor for the fan and a small D C pump for the means of water circulation, then install some solar electric PV modules to power the unit either on the roof, or on the top of the unit itself. Solar energy and air conditioning are a natural match.

"The time of day when air conditioning is most needed of course corresponds closely to the sunniest time; thus, it would be nice to use the sun to power air conditioners."

"And of the various ways devised to use the sun to cool air, PV-made electricity has one big advantage: it can substitute directly as the input power for existing air conditioners, so the AC industry does not have to make any major change to adopt a solar-powered electric unit."

OKay! Moving right along here is a very old concept we would like to give a good hard second look. Root cellars are nature's way of storing fruits and vegetables. And they can be excellent storage areas for other things as well. A hundred years ago root cellars were one of the few ways they had of keeping things cool. People not only put potatoes and carrots in their root cellars, but their preserved meat, milk and cream, fruits and vegetables - literally anything they needed to keep cool. Even though root cellars/storm shelters didn't get nearly as cold as a refrigerator during summer months, root cellars generally were and are 30 to 40 degrees F cooler than daytime summer temperatures. So just by adding a solar cooling device to a root cellar would in effect create a walk in cooler/freezer. Of course various chambers can be created to have different temperatures ideal for the select foods that are being stored there. As we were researching root cellars we came across this very interesting concept on the subject so here is the reference to, Green Home Building.

Alrighty then,

Okay! To the other side of the spectrum. Solar heating isn't a problem at all for any solar system, besides that is what the Sun does best is heat things up. The subject of solar heating begins again with a good passive solar design. Any good passive solar design will include thermal mass and properly placed, and sized glazing and as always good insulation. We talked earlier about radiant floors and their advantages. Radiant floors are a great idea, but of course you will need hot water and a pump to circulate it, to move the heat through the tubes to heat the space above the floor.

12/24 VOLT DC POWERED CIRCULATOR PUMP

This is where the solar hot water collector and a super insulated storage tank and a photovoltaic pump comes into play.

"But, what about those cold dark days in mid winter?"

You may ask? Well there are several ways to heat water without direct solar power and these should be installed as backup systems. We are talking a natural gas hot water heater combination with a wood burning furnace. During the year begin to collect firewood. If you are developing a wooded lot I'm sure this won't be a problem for several years.

If you live in a area where firewood is scarce then natural gas maybe your best option as a backup system. If this is the case I'd advice putting in extra insulation and increase thermal mass to help offset any extra heating cost. If you live in a forest as I do hardwoods are everywhere and need thinning out all the time as well large limps break off and fall to the ground after wind storms. Good forest maintenance and selective tree farming will keep your forest vibrant and healthy all throughout your whole lifetime to feed your wood burning furnace hot water heater systems. Thermo couples attached to a wood furnace. The thermo-couples begin producing a DC current when the furnace boiler reaches a surface temperature of 250° F. The current is used to maintain a battery charge to operate DC equipment or AC adaptive separate circuit. The furnace is also equipped with water heating thermosiphon circulating coil that subsidizes two flat plate solar collectors. During the colder seasons when outside temperature is lower and use patterns are usually highest, the extra space heating from carefully selected hardwood help to lower demands on other system components. We illustrate this relation superimposed over time with winter time use pattern. Related patterns based on a typical early spring day at the cabin using solar energy with outside temperature averaging 60 degrees. This method will maintain a well insulated 40 gallon tank at a average temperature of 115° F. What is so eloquent about this system is there are no pumps or the use of electricity to operate the system.

The sun's heat drives the solar collector as hot liquid rises it is displaced with the cooler liquid. The hotter the Sun' heat the faster the liquid travels around the loop. The same is true with the wood furnace. Heat drives the hot water around the system thus creating the thermosiphon effect. The furnace heats the water directly whereas a anti-freeze solution in a heat exchanger is used for the solar collectors due to the chance of freezing in the winter time.

Chapter Six

Transportation and Manufacturing Within the Solar Nation

We all love to travel. It is the very nature of the human spirit to explore. What is over that next hill? Where are my relatives? Or, I need a vacation! Well in these modern times the combustion engine is the most common way to transport the human body from one place to another but this is changing. In fact the emerging technologies of hydrogen fuel cells, hybrid vehicles, and solar electric cars and trucks as well bio diesel are very promising mold of transportation for the human family.

So before we go into all the details of constructing the total solar powered home lets talk about all these products and materials we will need to make the dwelling as well transporting them to the site. Of course we have to consider the pollution involved in manufacturing solar energy products and the mass distribution to sites where people are actually sitting up Enviro-Shelters. So lets explore some of the options, keeping in mind every thing you import onto your site from elsewhere has to get there through some medium of commerce. So first off, use local products as much as possible. Here in the south we have a lots of southern pine. For instance, so why should I dispatch a truck or train from California to bring me redwoods. Check your yellow pages and the internet for local suppliers that may have a lot of the items already in stock. More and more solar energy equipment is coming onto local markets every day. Most areas in the united states have local building supply warehouses as well plant nursery and as well seed stores, farmers markets,and exchanges. But still yet many products for a modern solar home will have to be ordered and shipped in such as, photovoltaic modules, storage tanks, pumps, inverters, and other system controls as well solar collectors, appliances and fixtures and others components. If at all possible order as much materials and equipment at one time to save a lot of trips, but if you are like a lot of folks you will be buying over time to keep from having to take out loans. Over the internet is a good place to buy goods and you will find many companies that supply solar products. For many crafty types many solar devices can be manufactured on site such as solar hot water collectors, attached greenhouses, solar ovens, distillers, fireplaces , vents, solar chimneys, solar heat grabbers, heat exchangers, and others.

You can usually find do it yourself plans for all these projects by searching over the internet or at a book store. Keep in mind everything man made is made somewhere and it took energy, time and materials from the Earth and People to make it. Someday soon many solar products will be made using the very solar power technology they are creating. Others facilities can be located near existing hydro-electric dams, Geo-thermal plants, wood chip boiler power plants, and solar furnaces, solar power towers, and others that are less polluting and environmentally friendly.

INTERNATIONAL SOLAR COMPETITIONS

Many solar industries can be located in wind farm areas to take advantage of prevailing winds. In fact in my view all photovoltaic modules manufactured should be installed on family homes or business immediately through some kind of home owner solar industry agreement plan with governmental incentives. Why pack away a solar electric device in a warehouse away from the SUN somewhere, when there are millions of rooftops awaiting to receive them right now! Magnetic levitation lightweight trains, trolleys, subways and cars will soon be commonplace throughout the world.

ELECTRIC VEHICLES

A secondary vehicle isolator battery charging systems are used year round for storing excess electricity while commuting in hybrid vehicles. The energy is transferred to dwelling by means of a special connector in garage area. The device will not drain cranking or drive battery system. Energy is on demand during high load hours in sequence with at home use patterns as well the storage amount saved in ampere hours needed during a up coming trip or daily commute mileage range. Excess energy from the home electrical system is diverted into the hybrid transportation reserve. The basic idea is to create a simple electric car system that can be operated within the arena of the solar electric community or village with either a battery exchange or other method of energy delivery system for cross country traveling. To make driving an electric car even more attractive (Unlimited Range Electric Car Systems) battery recharge/exchange stations were invented. In seconds the station automatically swaps batteries. You don't even have to get out of the car. Another very exciting emerging technology is the air car. Compressed air cars are powered by engines fueled by compressed air, which is stored in a tank at high pressure such as 30 MPa (4500 psi or 300 bar). Rather than driving engine pistons with an ignited fuel-air mixture, compressed air cars use the expansion of compressed air, in a similar manner to the expansion of steam in a steam engine. The question here is, can the compressed air be provided by solar or alternative energy? The answer is, yes making this technology a very promising adventure.

MAGNETIC LEVITATION TRACK SECTIONS

The propulsion systems for these magnetic tracks or roads will be energized by renewable natural fuels from local power plants, hydro-electric dams, and farms as well solar electricity positioned at key locations along the tracks and roads throughout the communities.

" We set out on the trail without the thought of a fuel other than the very highway beneath our feet. It is electrified! Beaming energy to the under carriage as needed automatically without a gesture or a command. The very atoms sense when electrons are needed. The motor less propulsion is as elegant as simple. A world without OIL is the greatest blessing Known , Yet unknown. The mother of invention is when nature is so beautiful it needs not to be invented again. Nature moves this whole universe in a instant, and spins this giant vehicle " Earth" around in just 24 hours.. That is fast enough to get us anywhere in no time flat. All the energy we will ever need is here all around us all the time. Once we quit digging for it. It appears out of thin air from the heavens. "

SOLAR ELECTRIC POWER STATION

Next lets talk about power tools. Power tools as you know have, and still are undergoing a revolution all over the world. Cordless and rechargeable power tools have evolved into a class, I'd call, " super tools." To start off a major solar construction project nothing is better than a good set of modern power tools on hand to do the job right and guess what? A Photovoltaic (PV) Direct current generating system can do the job. The PV Solar cells produce electricity year round.

The best season is between March 20 - September 23 intensifying during summer. Solar cells produce maximum energy during the hours of 9 a.m. - 4 p.m. on sunny days. Energy production is highest during low human demand use hours. This device is excellent for direct applications, (Cells wired directly to a DC load) or charging DC batteries for inverted AC electrical circuits during home time energy use hours. The PV average daily energy characteristics is superimposed on summer time human use pattern. Relationship of Photovoltaic output to pattern of energy use on a sunny day. The output can be adjusted to actual human demand usage by adding more PV modules until the desired electrical current is reached.

DC POWERED CORDLESS RECHARGEABLE TOOL KIT

A solar electric power station is a excellent way to power all these tools with a backup generator. Even though most cordless power tools are DC they use a AC powered recharger to recharge the batteries. A 40 amp solar electric system with a 2500 watt AC inverter will handle most applications for most of the smaller power tools and rechargeables. If you are operating large compressors and shop tools you may need to run a gasoline or natural gas operated generator just for that period they are in use. So plan ahead as many projects as possible and do the work in a safe and efficient manner.

AC TOOLS POWERED WITH THE AC INVERTER

This may include framing various structures within the Enviro-Shelter complex. A metal storage building is a good place to keep this equipment. In fact the roof of the metal building can be where the photovoltaic modules are located facing true south or on a passive solar tracking device near the construction site.

2500 WATT DC TO AC INVERTER

For those commuting back and forth to the job site. Many construction tools can be stored on the truck as well the on board engine alternator can recharge many batteries either direct DC, or thru a AC inverter mounted in the truck. Also remember that you need to match your A C inverter to your needs depending on your specific electrical loads and use patterns.

You may want a larger or smaller A C inverter. Be sure to upgrade your PV solar energy as needed. One thing that is so nice about solar energy is the module arrays and panels are easy to upgrade to any level. When you are done with construction just add your remote solar power station to your Enviro-Shelters for even more solar energy.

PASSIVE SOLAR TRACKER

As for other electronics modern builders use such as cell phones, digital camera, lap top computers, GPS devices, cam recorders, job site boom box, or electronic players, radios, walkie talkies, and rechargeable flashlights...etc, These are easily electrically maintained with a solar electric remote site system. Some may even be inclined to mount their portable solar power plants onto a utility trailer for easy transport between solar construction sites as temporary power is needed at each portable solar power plant.

Efficiency is also added by adding a sun tracking device to direct the array towards the incoming solar rays. One good solar direct application for instance is operating DC powered ventilation fans or DC pumps for evaporating cooling on hot summer days.

Solar Modular Home

The idea here is simple, a small totally solar powered portable home made in a factory similar to that of mobile home construction except these modules can be linked to form larger homes in time as the family expands or extra space is needed.

Okay , This isn't really what we are trying to accomplish here. Did you ever play with Legos? What about Lincoln logs? Well Imagine large real life size modules that interconnect, except they are a effusion of photovoltaic technology with modern plug and play technology rendering the whole structure energy independent. You know it takes a while before one can imagine that the whole global civilization is on the wrong path, a non renewable path and this has to change and change soon. Time and Time again this moment has happened in human history. Did the human beings of desperate times always make the right decisions? Well the answer is, NO. In fact most of the time people and governments as a whole make bad decisions. There are exceptions to this rule, and we are beginning to see some emerging.

We are beginning to see the New World emerge and it isn't about a lost religion, a false GOD, or obsolete science. It is about individuals taking the responsibility for their own lives in every aspect education, energy, shelter, nutrition, health, and wealth, with or without government or failed public programs, so called " educational systems" that basically brain wash humans to be consumers. One aspect of the future solar module homes you may not of imagined is the fact that the labor is done by the actual people that will live in the shelters. The Mobile Factory is a, " Do- IT- Yourself – Workshop " and the shelter comes with no mortgage or monthly payments.

From our Enviro-Shelter to yours may the sunshine shine into your heart the light of day.

The Emerging Solar Civilization

The advancing solar age of mankind is very rapidly becoming the reality as more and more human beings are experiencing in their communities all over the planet rapid change. In the United States of America, this reality is becoming the innovation of a nation. These are truly exciting times as many industries all across the country are gearing up for the future of electric hybrid cars, high tech solar homes, localized energy systems using combinations of wind, solar, wood, small hydroelectric, bio fuel and other renewable energy technologies, such as existing grid connecting devices that help eliminate battery storage.

Off Grid habitats, once just a dream has now again becoming the norms for many families that are moving back into the rural areas inspired by the concept of existing on this planet with a lifestyle that has a lighter carbon footprint. In summary, weighing the balance of present times and events, with increasing evidence of the degradation of the natural environment. In fact, the repercussions from unpredictable cause and effect responses from the Eco-system is an unstable environment. The massive dwindling of non-renewable, terribly polluting energy resources has already reached to levels that ecological compatible energy must be established to maintain sustainability. Therefore, the on going success of this experiment, and many other similar around the globe, is a growing testimony that the age of restoration is upon each of us. With this, the ultimate responsibility for the wholeness of the immediate environment, is truly in our own hands.

A Vision

www.ingramcontent.com/pod-product-compliance
Ingram Content Group UK Ltd.
Pitfield, Milton Keynes, MK11 3LW, UK
UKHW051135260726
13967UKWH00010B/3072